Song of the Flies

[An Account of the Events]

El canto de las moscas

[Versión de los acontecimientos]

poems by María Mercedes Carranza
with English translations
by Margarita Millar

Freedom Voices

Cover and book design:
Eliana P. Benavides Villegas
Cover art: Maestro Pedro Nel Góḿez,
detail *Dance of the Turkey Buzzards*
(La danza de los gallinazos)
Photograph of the cover illustration:
© Edwin Gómez Mesa

ISBN 978-0-915117-19-2
Published by Freedom Voices
P.O. Box 423115
San Francisco, CA 94142
www.freedomvoices.org
books@freedomvoices.org

Introduction

Canto de las Moscas (*Song of the Flies*), by the late Colombian poet María Mercedes Carranza, was published for the first time in 1997, following a decade marked by extremely high levels of violence in Colombia. At this point the country had already endured nearly half a century of armed struggle between government and rebel groups, and had more recently experienced the emergence of paramilitary forces and warring drug lords.

Carranza wrote these twenty-four poems, each bearing the name of a town or city that had been the site of large-scale violence, as a sort of chronicle and commemoration of the tragedies the people endured. The titles reflect a contradiction characteristic of Colombian reality: the beautifully-musical and whimsical place-names stand in cruel contrast to the events that marked them as massacre sites. Written in a form similar to Japanese haiku but not adhering to its strict line-and-syllable counts, the poems are short and spare.

Carranza's powerful work largely speaks for itself, but the elucidation of a few references may be helpful for readers unfamiliar with the Colombian context. For instance, "Canto 6/ Barrancabermeja" refers to a city in northeastern Colombia that takes its name from the reddish dirt of the Magdalena River banks along which it stands. Bermeja means red, calling to mind the blood that has run through Colombian rivers because the bodies of murder victims are commonly dumped there. In "Canto 9/ Segovia," the name Julio Daniel refers to poet and journalist Julio Daniel Chaparro, assassinated in that town in 1991. The name

Vista Hermosa (Beautiful View) in Canto 11 is of course particularly ironic, given the bleak and barren imagery of the poem. The "Flower War" in Canto 23 is a reference to ritualized Aztec warfare.

Carranza was born in 1945, in Bogotá. She was a widely-respected figure in Colombia: a cultural journalist, member of the National Assembly, and founder-director of the Casa de Poesía Silva in Bogotá, an organization which advanced the creation, nurturance and dissemination of poetry. Her overarching passion, in a passionately-lived life, was her art. She believed in the power of poems to change and heal a country that had endured seemingly endless murder, truncated lives, unfulfilled dreams, and unspeakable levels of brutality.

In May of 2003, María Mercedes Carranza put out a call for poetry submissions for an annual poetry festival in Colombia, with the theme of "Let's Lay War to Rest." She received over 30,000 poems from Colombians clamoring desperately for peace. This overwhelming response, filled with anguish about the situation in the country, that she herself had written about, may have been too much to bear. Carranza committed suicide in July 2003. The events that preceded her death are a moving and painful illustration of the destructive connection between violence and personal life in Colombia.

Canto de las Moscas / *Song of the Flies*, dedicated to the slain presidential candidate Luis Carlos Galán, stands as a timeless testament to both the poet's power and impotence in the face of devastating violence.

It is a pleasure to present this new bilingual edition in honor of María Mercedes Carranza's contribution to the poetry of Colombia and the world.

Song of the Flies

[An Account of the Events]

To Luis Carlos: always

Canto 1

NECOCLÍ

Quizás
el próximo instante
de noche tarde o mañana
en Necoclí
se oirá nada más
el canto de las moscas.

Canto 1

NECOCLÍ

Maybe
this next instant
late at night or in the morning
in Necoclí
only the song of the flies
will be heard.

Canto 2

MAPIRIPÁN

Quieto el viento,
    el tiempo.
Mapiripán es ya
    una fecha.

Canto 2

MAPIRIPÁN

Still wind,
  still time.
Mapiripán is now
  a date.

Canto 3

A Mario Rivero

TAMBORALES

Bajo
el siseo sedoso
del platanal
alguien
sueña que vivió.

Canto 3

To Mario Rivero

TAMBORALES

Under
the silky hissing
of the banana forest
somebody
dreams he lived.

Canto 4

DABEIBA

El río es dulce aquí
        en Dabeiba
y lleva rosas rojas
esparcidas en las aguas.
        No son rosas,
        es la sangre
que toma otros caminos.

Canto 4

DABEIBA

The river is sweet here
            in Dabeiba
and carries red roses
scattered over its waters.
            They are not roses,
            but blood
following other courses.

Canto 5

ENCIMADAS

Bajo la tierra de Encimadas
   el terror fulgura aún
   en los ojos florecidos
sobre la tierra de Encimadas.

Canto 5

ENCIMADAS

Under the earth of Encimadas
    terror still glows
    in the eyes in bloom
over the earth of Encimadas.

Canto 6

BARRANCABERMEJA

Entre el cielo y el suelo
            yace
pálida Barrancabermeja.
            Diríase
la sangre desangrada.

Canto 6

BARRANCABERMEJA

Between heaven and earth
lies
pale Barrancabermeja.
as if
blood bled to death.

Canto 7

TIERRALTA

Esto es la boca que hubo,
esto los besos.
Ahora sólo tierra: tierra
entre la boca quieta.

Canto 7

TIERRALTA

This is the mouth that once was,
          these the kisses.
Now there is only dirt
  inside that still mouth.

Canto 8

EL DONCELLO

El asesino danza
la Danza de la Muerte.
A cada paso suyo
          alguien cae
sobre su propia sombra.

Canto 8

EL DONCELLO

The murderer dances
the Dance of Death.
At each step
                someone tumbles
over his own shadow.

Canto 9

SEGOVIA

Los versos
de Julio Daniel
son la risa
del Gato de Cheshire
en el aire de Segovia.

Canto 9

SEGOVIA

The poems
of Julio Daniel
are the Cheshire Cat's
smile
in Segovia's air.

Canto 10

AMAIME

En Amaime
los sueños se cubren
de tierra como
si fueran podredumbre.

Canto 10

AMAIME

In Amaime
dreams are covered
with dirt
as if they were carrion.

Canto 11

VISTA HERMOSA

El alto tallo
  espectral,
quemada, yerta,
    solitaria
flor del páramo.
    Así
Vista Hermosa.

Canto 11

VISTA HERMOSA

The tall stalk
        spectral,
burned, rigid,
        lonesome
flower of the high plains.
            This is
Vista Hermosa.

Canto 12

PÁJARO

Si la mar es el morir
        en Pájaro
la vida sabe a mar.

Canto 12

PÁJARO

If the sea is death,
        in Pájaro
life tastes of the sea.

Canto 13

URIBIA

Cae un cuerpo
        y otro cuerpo.
Toda la tierra
sobre ellos pesa.

Canto 13

URIBIA

One body falls
        and then another.
They bear the weight
of the whole earth.

Canto 14

CONFINES

Lluvia y silencio
es el mundo en
          Confines.
Desolación de páramo.

Canto 14

CONFINES

Rain and silence
are the world of
        Confines.
Desolation of the high plains.

Canto 15

CALDONO

¿Quien
llega a Caldono enciende
el fuego fatuo
y convoca
a los gusanos?

Canto 15

CALDONO

Do those who come
to Caldono light
the foxfire
and summon
the worms?

Canto 16

HUMADEA

Ve a
Humadea y mira
sus calles de aire:
ríos rojos repletos
de garzas blancas.
Ríos quietos.

Canto 16

HUMADEA

Go to
Humadea and see
its streets made of air:
red rivers full to the brim with
white herons.
Still rivers.

Canto 17

PORE

En Pore la muerte
pasa de mano en mano.
        La muerte:
carne de la tierra.

Canto 17

PORE

In Pore death
moves from hand to hand.
          Death:
flesh of the earth.

Canto 18

PAUJIL

Estallan las flores sobre
la tierra
de Paujil. En las corolas
aparecen las bocas
de los muertos.

Canto 18

PAUJIL

Flowers burst open over
    the soil
of Paujil. In their corollas
appear the mouths
    of the dead.

Canto 19

SOTAVENTO

Como las nubes,
        la muerte
hoy en Sotavento:
Difunta blancura.

Canto 19

SOTAVENTO

Death is
   like the clouds
in Sotavento today:
lifeless whiteness.

Canto 20

ITUANGO

El viento
ríe en las mandíbulas
de los muertos.
En Ituango,
el cadáver de la risa.

Canto 20

ITUANGO

The wind
laughs in the jaws
of the dead.
In Ituango,
the corpse of laughter.

Canto 21

TARAIRA

En Taraira
el recuerdo de la vida
duele.
Mañana
será tierra y olvido.

Canto 21

TARAIRA

In Taraira
the memory of life
hurts.
Tomorrow
it will be dust and oblivion.

Canto 22

MIRAFLORES

Caen los cuerpos
            en Miraflores
caen los sueños.
            Miraflores:
cementerio de sueños.

Canto 22

MIRAFLORES

Bodies fall
		in Miraflores
dreams fall.
		Miraflores:
cemetery of dreams.

Canto 23

CUMBAL

En bluyines
y con la cara pintada
llegó la muerte
        a Cumbal.
Guerra Florida
a filo de machete.

Canto 23

CUMBAL

In blue jeans
and a painted face
death came
            to Cumbal.
The Flower War
at machete point.

Canto 24

SOACHA

Un pájaro
negro husmea
las sobras de
la vida.
Puede ser Dios
o el asesino:
da lo mismo ya.

Canto 24

SOACHA

A black bird
pecks at
the remains of
life.
It could be God
or the murderer:
it doesn't matter now.

About the Translator

Margarita Millar, a native of Colombia, lives in San Francisco since 1983, where she obtained an M.A. in Comparative Literature at San Francisco State University. Ms. Millar has worked for 15 years as a professional interpreter and translator. She continues to translate the poetic works of María Mercedes Carranza and other contemporary Latin American and American authors.

To the translation of *Song of the Flies [An Account of the Events]*, Norma Kaminsky and Christy Rodgers contributed as editors, researchers and translation consultants.

Other Works by María Mercedes Carranza

Vainas y otros poemas
Tengo miedo
Hola, soledad
Maneras del desamor
De amor y desamor